THE
HONORABLE
MENTIONS

RYAN
GEORGE
KITTLEMAN

Half A Library
© 2022
ISBN: 978-0-9849575-4-5

THE TAVERN

They drank   again and again.

wine   poured,

        insults   uttered,

                      songs   sung,

        clothing

                      removed,

manners   banished,

        from all   but a few.

The tavern   is   closing   soon.

Some *broke:*

                      into the   tomb

                      regaling the   dead

              with

        cheese,

                      tobacco,   and

                      strong   beer.

Some *ran:*

                into the   streets

    yelling,

                screaming,

                        banging

                on doors,

      knocking   over

                trash   cans.

Some *wondered:*

    why were they incapable

        of having a good time

                like the others?

They drank   again

            and again.

                There was no peace.

A dark storm was brewing.

                    One man: *tossed*

out the window

in a fit of passion.

                                  One man: *hung*

                from the ceiling

just to see his face turn blue.

                There was a surplus of heartache.

They drank   again

                      and again

                                  and again.

                They amused themselves by:

breaking: windows.

                They amused themselves by:

eating: coals,

chewing: brimstone,

licking: pokers,

broiling: meat   on their   tongues.

                There was no escape.

The tavern   is   closing   soon.

MIXED REVIEWS

The   artist:

        gave:

                a preview

        of:

                his latest work.

The   guest:

        left:

                unimpressed.

BLUE SMOKE

when touched

      the bombardier beetle

            produces a

        blue smoke

its chief defense

          against its enemies.

        blue smoke

now rolling

      into the room

         denser than before.

its odor

           burning feathers

VILLAGE GOSSIP

The *affair:*

      commenced : in : a cabbage garden

      (behind the house)

The *widows:*

      hurried : to : watch

      (behind the curtains)

The *women:*

      exposed : much : pale flesh

      (to warm rays)

The *men:*

      walked : across : a field

      (of raw eggs)

      despite :

      (considerable planning)

The *affair:*

      went :   (terribly wrong)

KEEPING TIME – I

6 o'clock. – Beef too boiled, beer a little stale.

8 o'clock. – Into the paddock, above the dale.

10 o'clock. – Lunch with Rose, very pale.

11 o'clock. – Hand squeezed, thrice.

3 o'clock. – House burned, twice.

5 o'clock. – ???

8 o'clock. – Nap.

PERFORMANCE ANXIETY

The musician was playing at the   b

          o

          t

            t

              o

                m

of a lake.

His house

had burned,

twice

already.

"Such a cruel world this is, no?"

His performance

had ended,

twice

already.

He tore the laurel from his brow

Her words:

"More than ever, darling, I adore you."

He tore the laurel to pieces:

"Such a cruel world this is, no?"

KEEPING TIME – II

He   ATE

FOUR meals each   day

                   each lasting   ONE hour

He   then   SMOKED

FOR   the next   EIGHT hours

He   then   SLEPT

FOR   the next   TWELVE

                each   night

He   FALLS

upon his   bed,

                           DRAGGING

His   ball   and chain.

"The bed is grief's first refuge,"

he'd say.

ANALYSIS

To dream
of swimming
in a river

of rice-beer
causes incontinence.

To dream
of a rope
which does not
break
causes hypertension.

To dream
of being pursued
with a sharp
weapon
causes flatulence.

To dream
of being wounded
and bleeding
freely
causes gout.

HANG UPS – I

Show me a stone,
and my nose
will bleed.

Show me a rose,
and I will faint.

The sound of a broom
makes me ill.

The sound of a violin
makes me tremble,
all over.

(_____)

If a man is	(killed)	
aboard a	(ship),	
the	(killer) is to be	(bound)
to the	(dead body) and	
	(thrown) into the	(sea).

If a man is	(killed)	
on	(land),	
the	(killer) is to be	(bound)
to the	(dead body) and	
	(buried) in the	(leaves).

HANG UPS – II

I was bitten by a tarantula,

(rare)

and suffered an attack of delirium

every year thereafter.

(medium rare)

If music plays,

I imagine the tarantula

has stung me again.

(medium well)

If music plays,

I imagine the tarantula

going to a pump,

removing its wig,

and sluicing its head

with water.

(well done)

THE CIRCUS – I

This evening,

        and during the Summer Season,

                I will perform

           several new exercises

of Rope-dancing,

      Tumbling,

          Vaulting,

             Ladder-dancing,

               and Balancing.

This evening,

        and during the Spring Season,

                I will perform

           a new Grand Dance

called

      Apollo

           and

                Daphne.

This evening,

        and during the Fall Season,

                I will perform

              several imitations

of the lark,

      thrush,

         blackbird,

           goldfinch,

             and canary-bird.

This evening,

and during the Winter Season,

I will perform

a Sailor's Pantomime

reenacting a great battle,

the dramatic wrecking of a bridge,

and the drowning of all
hope.

THE CIRCUS – II

I will bend

an iron poker

over my arm,

and another

around my neck

(!)

I will lift

a table

with my teeth

(!!)

I will lift

a butt*full

of water

(!!!)

Admission:

one coin   per loin

1 butt = 2 hogsheads = approximately 150 gallons

THE CIRCUS – III

CONTEST!

the ugliest grinner

will

be

the

winner!

Admission:

one fin   per grin

THE CIRCUS – IV

The old man	The old woman
drew a small pipe	drew magic letters
from his pocket	on her palm
and began to play	and began to pray

Admission:

FREE

CHAPTER V

The Vision

in Leather.

The Vision

in _____.

The Vision

in _____.

&c.

∞

THE SHIP

is   a

sieve.

THE OARS

are   not

shoulder

blades.

∞

GO!

Go

Go and

        Go and   Go

        Go and

                        Go and

try

                        Go and

        Go and

try

        your luck

                        Go

                        Go!

∞

One by one,

the torches vanished

from the rooftops.

There was nothing left

to protect.

∞

The veil

is impenetrable

to our gaze.

∞

About

Ryan Kittleman is an artist and writer living in San Francisco. His paintings have been exhibited at the Crocker Art Museum, Morris Graves Museum of Art, and the Museum of Northern California Art, among others. In addition to *The Honorable Mentions*, Ryan is the author of two novels, *The Great Peace* and *The High Cost of Macaroni*.

www.ingramcontent.com/pod-product-compliance
Lightning Source LLC
Chambersburg PA
CBHW060544030426
42337CB00021B/4416